YOU CHOOSE

CAN YOU ESCAPE A HAUNTED MUSEUM?

An Interactive Paranormal Adventure

by Megan Cooley Peterson

CAPSTONE PRESS
a capstone imprint

Published by Capstone Press, an imprint of Capstone
1710 Roe Crest Drive, North Mankato, Minnesota 56003
capstonepub.com

Copyright © 2026 by Capstone. All rights reserved. No part of this
publication may be reproduced in whole or in part, or stored in a retrieval
system, or transmitted in any form or by any means, electronic, mechanical,
photocopying, recording, or otherwise, without written permission of the
publisher.

Library of Congress Cataloging-in-Publication Data is available on the
Library of Congress website.
ISBN: 9798875210297 (hardcover)
ISBN: 9798875210266 (paperback)
ISBN: 9798875210273 (ebook PDF)

Summary: Readers explore haunted museums around the world and experience
paranormal activity that has been inspired by reports from real people.

Editorial Credits
Editor: Mandy Robbins; Designer: Elijah Blue; Media Researcher: Jo Miller;
Production Specialist: Tori Abraham

Image Credits
Alamy: Uwe Deffner, 62; Getty Images: Archive Photos, 45, CribbVisuals,
75, duncan1890, 6, 38, Hulton Archive, 14, iStock/gmnicholas, 102, Marc
Piasecki, 9, Pawel Libera/LightRocket, 28; Library of Congress: Prints &
Photographs Division, 35; Shutterstock: Artem Avetisyan, 43, Benjamin B,
56, breakermaximus, cover (frames), Everett Collection, 83, EWY Media,
57, FOTOKITA, cover (hand), Hugh K Telleria, 94, Inked Pixels, 72, Jaroslav
Moravcik, 106, Kiselev Andrey Valerevich, 32, Kit Leong, 82, Mistervlad,
16, Olena Tatarintseva, 61, Renata Sedmakova, 40, RozenskiP, 78, Zhukova
Valentyna, 18; Superstock: Piemags/PL Photography Limited, 51

Design Elements
Capstone: Dina Her; Shutterstock: Boyan Dimitrov, carlos castilla,
Nik Merkulov, Olha Nion, Runrun2

Any additional websites and resources referenced in this book are not
maintained, authorized, or sponsored by Capstone. All product and company
names are trademarks™ or registered® trademarks of their respective holders.

TABLE OF CONTENTS

INTRODUCTION
About Your Adventure............5

CHAPTER 1
A Haunting Choice 7

CHAPTER 2
The Louvre 19

CHAPTER 3
The British Museum 47

CHAPTER 4
The Smithsonian................79

CHAPTER 5
Haunted Museums 103

    More Ghostly Encounters.........106
    Other Paths to Explore 108
    Glossary......................109
    Select Bibliography 110
    Read More....................111
    Internet Sites 111
    About the Author 112

INTRODUCTION
ABOUT YOUR ADVENTURE

YOU are a novelist writing a book about a museum curator who fights evil. You're about to visit a museum for research. Rumors swirl that it is haunted! What will you do if you have a ghostly encounter at a museum?

Chapter One sets the scene. Then you choose which path to read. Follow the directions at the bottom of the page. The decisions you make will change your outcome. After you finish one path, go back and read the others for new perspectives and more adventures.

Turn the page to begin your adventure.

CHAPTER 1
A HAUNTING CHOICE

Click!

The night security guard at your local museum locks the doors behind you. You stayed past closing time doing research for your novel. He practically had to shove you out the door. Your story takes place at a museum. It follows a secret society of magical curators. They use the world's most priceless objects to protect humanity from evil.

Turn the page.

The problem is that your small-town museum won't make a very exciting setting for your novel. You have connections at a couple of famous museums. You hope to travel to them for research. Maybe you could use these museums as backdrops for your story.

As you walk home, you stop at the library. You're not ready to go home yet, and it's still open for another hour. One day, maybe your novel will sit on one of these shelves.

You settle in at one of the large tables and turn on your laptop. You've always wanted to visit the famous Louvre Museum in Paris, France. You have a cousin who works there, and she's offered to show you around. As you research, you learn the Louvre was built on the site of a fortress built in the 1100s. A fortress turned museum would be a perfect setting for your book!

Over the years, the Louvre was expanded to be a home for royalty. Then, in 1793, the Louvre became a palace museum. Today, many pieces reside there. Millions of people visit the famous portrait *Mona Lisa* by Leonardo da Vinci each year.

The *Mona Lisa* by Leonardo da Vinci

Turn the page.

The sky outside the library windows darkens. Dark clouds blow in, and lightning flashes. You wait for the thunder that's sure to follow. But you're distracted by the sound of footsteps behind you. When you turn around, there's no one there.

In fact, you seem to be the only patron in the library. And you swear there were people here when you arrived.

"Hello?" you call out.

The footsteps continue. You begin to pack up your stuff. Just as you push in your chair, something jumps out from behind a bookshelf. You gasp. Then you recognize who it is and roll your eyes.

"Real nice, Colin," you say. "You scared me!"

Colin is your best friend. He works at the library. You had forgotten he might be here.

"Sorry! I couldn't resist." He sits down and looks at your laptop. "Research for your novel?"

You nod. "I was thinking the Louvre might be a great place to visit."

"Does your book have any ghosts in it?" Colin asks.

You frown. "Why do you ask?" He knows your book is about magic and monsters and that you're a little afraid of ghosts. Your older cousin used to tell terrifying ghost stories during family vacations at the lake.

Colin gives you a look. "Because it's totally haunted, that's why. You might want to dig a little deeper."

Turn the page.

Your friend is right. You find many stories of hauntings at the Louvre. The ghost of Jean l'Ecorcheur, or Jack the Skinner, makes your skin crawl. Legends say he was a butcher who was close with France's Queen Catherine in the 1500s. Stories say he killed her political rivals on her orders. But he knew too much, and she had him killed. His ghost allegedly still haunts the Louvre and its gardens. He is often seen dressed in red. His ghost is called "The Red Man of the Tuileries."

When the library closes, the two of you walk to a nearby pizzeria for dinner. The rain has lightened, so you don't get too soaked.

As you wait for your food, you continue researching museums. Your great-aunt used to work at the British Museum in London, England. The museum opened in 1759. Today, there are about 8 million objects there.

One of the most famous objects housed there is the Rosetta Stone. Historians used this stone to decipher ancient Egyptian hieroglyphs. Ancient Egypt is your favorite era of history to study. You'd love to include some Egyptian objects in your novel.

The British Museum also has plenty of ghostly stories. A dog statue is said to come alive at night. The museum's fire alarms go off for no apparent reason. And invisible hands shove people. You swallow. With so much history, you're not surprised by the number of ghostly stories. But could any of them be true?

"You alright?" Colin asks. "You look as though you've seen a ghost."

"If I ever see a ghost, I'll probably faint," you admit.

Turn the page.

Colin swipes the last slice of pizza. "My sister just got a job at the Smithsonian," he says. "Maybe you could visit there?"

Your heart beats faster as you research the Smithsonian in Washington, D.C. Founded in 1846, the museum was named for British scientist James Smithson. He left his estate to the United States after he died in 1829. He asked that a place of learning be founded in his name.

James Smithson

The first building constructed was called the Castle. It was made of red sandstone and completed in 1855. When Smithson died, he was buried in Genoa, Italy. In 1904, his remains were moved to a crypt inside the Castle.

"Please tell me it isn't haunted," you say. Your stomach feels a little queasy.

Colin leans toward you. "My sister has heard stories. Apparently, there are all kinds of ghosts wandering around."

"But has your sister actually *seen* any ghosts?"

He shrugs. "Not yet, but she hasn't been there very long."

Your shoulders slump. Every museum you want to visit is said to be haunted. But maybe the rumors aren't true. You can't know until you visit them. Firsthand experience at these museums would make your novel that much stronger.

"Are you sure you can handle a visit to a haunted museum?" Colin asks.

Thunder booms, and you accidentally knock over your glass of soda. Your friend can't stop laughing.

- To explore the Louvre in France, turn to page 19.
- To visit the British Museum in London, turn to page 47.
- To go to the Smithsonian in Washington, D.C., turn to page 79.

CHAPTER 2
THE LOUVRE

You pack your bags and hop a flight to Paris, France. During your flight, you do more research. In 1190, France's King Philip Augustus built a fortress to protect Paris from invaders. It sat along the River Seine. It had a moat and guard towers.

As the city grew, the fortress became too small. In 1528, King Francis I built a grand palace in its place. He invited artists such as Leonardo da Vinci to his court. French rulers added onto the palace over the years. Many brought in priceless works of art.

Turn the page.

In 1793, the French government opened the Louvre as a public museum. Today, the Louvre is the world's most popular art museum. Parts of the old fortress's foundation can be viewed in the Louvre's basement.

Tucked inside your backpack is another stack of papers. As you flip through them, you realize they are about the so-called hauntings. You didn't print these.

Colin must have put them there, you think. You might as well read them.

Jack the Skinner is said to haunt the Louvre's gardens. But as you read, you learn the museum's interior has its own ghostly residents. The museum houses many ancient Egyptian artifacts. One of the mummies is said to come alive after dark. It roams the hallways, looking for victims.

Another ghostly visitor is a French soldier who died in 1815. His ghost is said to admire paintings of French emperor Napoleon Bonaparte. The idea of a lonely, ghostly soldier makes you a bit sad.

When you arrive in Paris, you take a taxi to the museum. The City of Light glitters. You spot famous landmarks like the Notre-Dame Cathedral and Eiffel Tower.

When you arrive at the Louvre, it's 6:30 p.m. The museum has already closed for the day. But your cousin Jules is waiting for you at the glass pyramid entrance. She's taking you on a special after-hours tour.

"Welcome to Paris!" Jules says and gives you a big hug.

Turn the page.

You spend a few minutes catching up. Then she gives you two choices. You can tour the museum's Tuileries Gardens first or go inside right away.

The Louvre itself is massive. The former palace has huge wings that wrap around two courtyards. The one you're standing in has the giant glass pyramid entrance. Just past the courtyard are the gardens. The green space is huge and filled with flowers and trees.

- To explore the gardens first, go to page 23.
- To tour the inside of the Louvre, turn to page 27.

Jules takes you into the Tuileries Gardens. In 1564, Queen Catherine commissioned the building of a new palace and gardens right next to the Louvre. Both were named after tile factories that had stood there, called tuileries. The palace burned down in 1871. It was never rebuilt. That same year, the gardens were opened to the public.

The vast gardens have three sections. The Grand Carré is closest to the Louvre building. It has ponds and many flower beds in bloom.

"This is my favorite part of the garden," Jules tells you.

You bend down to smell a flower. Someone whispers behind you. You turn around, but there's no one there. You ask your cousin if she heard it too.

Turn the page.

23

"Heard what?" she asks.

Suddenly, the whispering returns.

"I'll get you next!" says a raspy voice.

You look all around you, but Jules is the only person nearby.

Jules's eyes grow wide. "I heard it that time," she says. "It might be the ghost of Jack the Skinner! I've heard stories that his ghost threatens guests. But I didn't believe it . . . until now!"

Goose bumps have broken out on your arm. Is the ghost of Jack the Skinner really in the garden?

"Maybe we should move onto the next section of the garden," Jules suggests. You're happy to follow her.

The Grand Couvert has eight groves of trees. The trees tower above you. They almost put that strange whispering out of your mind. When Jules's phone rings, you startle.

"It's my boss," she tells you. "I'll meet you at the pyramid." She answers the call and walks toward the pyramid.

You continue walking through the trees by yourself. At this hour, there aren't many people in the garden. You like the idea of your book characters spending time in a garden like this. As you're admiring a particularly tall tree, you notice a man up ahead. He's dressed all in red. His clothing is old-fashioned. You have a strange feeling about him.

- To follow the man in red, turn to page 26.
- To find your cousin inside the pyramid, turn to page 27.

You meander through the garden, a few steps behind the man. But no matter how fast you walk, you never seem to get any closer. He's probably just a tourist like you who wants to be left alone. You're about to turn back, but then he walks directly through a tree trunk! You blink and rub your eyes.

I must be tired from the plane ride, you tell yourself. *People can't walk through trees.*

You find your cousin standing near the pyramid entrance. She waves to you. You could go inside with her. But you're still curious about the man in red. Could it really be the ghost of Jack the Skinner? Including a ghost in your story might make it more exciting. Still, your fear of ghosts makes you question following him.

- To meet your cousin at the pyramid, go to page 27.
- To continue following the man, turn to page 42.

You follow your cousin inside the museum's glass and metal pyramid entrance. The pyramid rises from the museum's gravel courtyard.

Jules tells you about its history. The pyramid was designed by Chinese-American architect I.M. Pei and completed in 1989. It leads underground into a courtyard, connecting the wings of the Louvre.

As you follow Jules below, the temperature drops. Goose bumps break out on your arms. The space is huge. Without any other people around, it is eerily quiet.

Jules takes you into the Sully Wing of the museum. It houses ancient Greek and Egyptian art and objects. Soon, you arrive at the Egyptian exhibit. A large statue sits outside the entrance, and you stare up at it in awe.

Turn the page.

"This is the Great Sphinx of Tanis," Jules explains. "It's half-human, half-animal. It was made of pink granite between 2620 BC and 1866 BC and came to the Louvre in 1826."

The Great Sphinx of Tanis

Next, you stop in front of a sarcophagus on display. This coffin is shaped like a person and painted gold. It even has a face. Hieroglyphs cover the lid. Many ancient Egyptians were mummified and buried in these coffins. Some were also buried with items they might need in the next life.

A cool breeze flits across your neck. You get a sudden chill. When you turn to ask Jules about a draft, she's gone!

"Jules?" you say. She doesn't answer. Your phone suddenly doesn't have any service either.

Scriiiiiitch.

You slowly turn back to the display case. The lid of the sarcophagus appears to be moving!

- To run away, turn to page 30.
- To duck behind another display, turn to page 32.

Racing through the Egyptian exhibit, you shake the fear that the statues will come to life. Soon, you find yourself in a long gallery. Paintings hang on red walls.

In your novel, the main character often paces the gallery to think. You do the same and take some deep breaths. You notice your phone is working again. You text Jules and ask where she went. She asks you the same thing and agrees to meet you. Whatever you saw in the Egyptian exhibit must have been your imagination.

You stop in front of a huge painting called *Coronation of the Emperor*. It shows Napoleon Bonaparte at the Notre-Dame Cathedral in 1804. Napoleon was a famous French ruler and military leader.

Soon, your cousin Jules joins you. "There you are," she says, a bit out of breath. "Where did you run off to?"

"The sarcophagus lid started to move," you say. "And I couldn't find you!"

Jules makes a face. "That's odd," she says. "I was there the entire time. I called after you, but you must not have heard me."

You shudder and turn back to the painting. As you admire the artwork, your skin grows clammy. The room is so cold, you can see your breath. You slowly turn toward Jules.

Only it's not your cousin standing next to you. It's a man dressed in a military uniform. He stares up at the painting. And he's almost see-through!

- To gather your courage and speak to the ghostly soldier, turn to page 34.
- To scream in fear, turn to page 38.

You peer around the display case you've hidden behind. A gnarled hand slides the sarcophagus lid off. A mummy slowly sits up. Its body is wrapped in dirty-looking gauze. When the mummy stands, some of the gauze falls away from its face. It has shriveled black skin and sunken eyes. You can hardly believe it!

The mummy smashes out of its glass display case. The glass shatters, and the mummy climbs out! A chemical smell fills your nostrils. You feel relief as the mummy ambles in the opposite direction.

But then you remember your cousin is still out there somewhere! What if the mummy tries to hurt her?

You spot Jules at the end of the hall. Her back is turned toward the mummy. You try to text her a warning, but your phone has run out of battery. You were certain it was fully charged only moments ago.

- To try to distract the mummy and save your cousin, turn to page 36.
- To go for help, turn to page 40.

The ghost is dressed in a blue and white uniform. He flickers as he stares up at the massive painting. That's when you notice he's crying.

"Are you alright?" you ask. Your voice trembles.

The ghost faces you. "I fought in the Battle of Waterloo," he says. His voice is deep and crackling. "But I fear I did not make it off the battlefield."

You read about the Battle of Waterloo. Fought in 1815, it was Napoleon's final defeat by the British. It marked the end of France's takeover of Europe.

The ghost wipes the phantom tears from his eyes. "It was my dying wish to see my leader's portrait one final time."

The ghostly soldier salutes the painting. Then he slowly fades away. In his place stands your cousin.

"You are not going to believe what just happened!" you tell Jules excitedly. You can't wait to put this character in your novel.

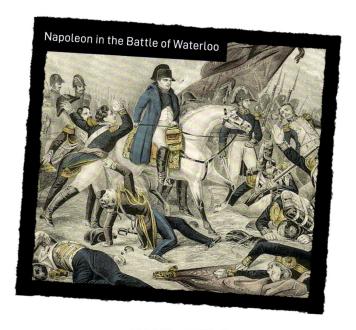
Napoleon in the Battle of Waterloo

THE END

To follow another path, turn to page 16.
To learn more about haunted museums, turn to page 103.

You jump out from your hiding spot. "Here I am!" you shout. "Come and get me!"

The mummy jerks to a stop. It looks at you over its decaying shoulder. Its eye holes glow red. Its sharp teeth glint like knives.

Your cousin turns around just as the mummy starts limping toward you. Before you know what's happening, the mummy starts to run. How is it so fast?

You turn and run in the opposite direction. You pump your legs as hard as you can. But you can barely breathe.

The mummy's fingers graze the back of your T-shirt. You fall to the ground and cover your head with your arms.

It's all over. You'll never leave the Louvre alive.

"Are you okay?" Jules asks.

She's standing over you. You're lying in front of the mummy display. The sarcophagus lid remains closed. Did you imagine it? You tell her about the mummy and how it chased you.

"Let me buy you a coffee," she says. "You need it."

As you drink your coffee, Jules tells you the legend of the Louvre's cursed mummy. "Stories say the mummy sneaks out of its display at night. I've never seen it. But I think you just did!"

As you leave the museum, you still feel the mummy's fingers on your shirt. This memory will haunt you forever.

THE END

To follow another path, turn to page 16.
To learn more about haunted museums, turn to page 103.

A bloodcurdling scream tears out of you. To your shock, the soldier screams too! Then his ghost stumbles into you. Your entire body goes cold. It feels as if you've stepped into a cold mist.

The light in the room changes. You're no longer in a gallery at the Louvre. You're inside the Notre-Dame Cathedral. You recognize the regal man standing only feet from you. It's Napoleon Bonaparte!

Napoleon Bonaparte

You look down and find yourself dressed in a fancy robe. Your arms and legs look strange, almost . . . painted on.

Horror grows in your chest as you realize where you are. You're trapped inside the painting of Napoleon's coronation! Terrified, you step forward and tumble onto the ground.

You're back in the gallery. The ghostly soldier is gone. Jules stares at you in shock. You wonder if you really stepped into a painting or if it was just a dream. Either way, you're ready to leave this museum.

THE END

To follow another path, turn to page 16.
To learn more about haunted museums, turn to page 103.

You can't save Jules on your own. There must be a security guard who can help. You just need to find them.

As you run through the maze of the Louvre, you get all turned around. You have no idea where you are. You find a map on a nearby wall. It tells you that you're still in the Egyptian exhibit.

"No, that can't be right," you say out loud. You've been wandering for at least half an hour. You turn to run but accidentally trip over something. You fall to the ground. Everything goes dark.

When you wake up, it's still dark. You try to sit up, but your head hits something solid. You try to move your arms and legs. But you're trapped in a small, enclosed space. It's hot and smells of dust and old dirt. You are stuck inside the sarcophagus! You try to push off the lid, but it won't budge. No one hears you scream. Overwhelmed with fear, you pass out. Hopefully you wake up to find this all to be a nightmare.

THE END

To follow another path, turn to page 16.
To learn more about haunted museums, turn to page 103.

The man in red disappears around a large statue. You dash through the trees to follow him.

The light in the garden changes. It was late afternoon when you arrived. Now it's dark. Stars twinkle in the sky. How long have you been out here? You reach for your phone. But it's not in your pocket! Your clothing is different too.

Suddenly, you spot the man in red standing next to a woman. She wears a poofy gown and an odd headdress. She looks royal. Is this a re-enactment? You want to shout for your cousin, but something tells you not to.

You crouch down as several men with swords surround the man in red.

"Goodbye, Jack," the woman says. She waves her hand, as if giving a signal. The guards attack the man in red!

Turn the page.

The Tuileries Garden at night

A chill crawls up your back as you recognize this woman from your research. It's Queen Catherine! Catherine was born in Italy. She was raised by Catholic nuns after her parents died. She married France's King Henry II in 1533.

You feel a sneeze coming on and try to hold it back, but you can't help it. Your allergies are acting up.

Ah-choo!

The queen's eyes snap toward you. "You're next, dear," she says, and you faint.

When you wake up, you're lying in the garden. The sun has not yet set. The stars are gone. Your cousin is splashing water on your face.

"Are you alright?" Jules asks. You tell her about the queen and the man in red.

Queen Catherine of France

"I can't believe the legend is true," she says.

But you can. You'll never forget your haunting time at the Louvre.

THE END

To follow another path, turn to page 16.
To learn more about haunted museums, turn to page 103.

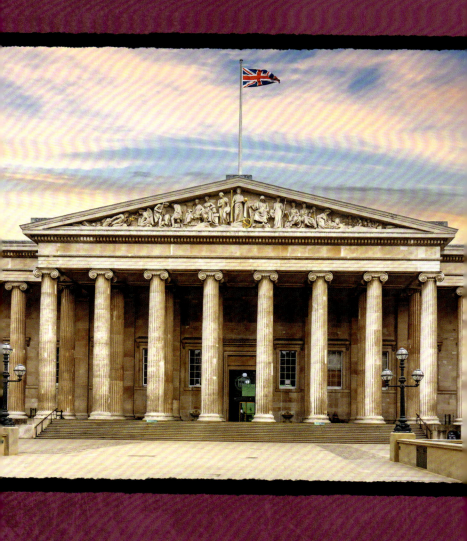

CHAPTER 3
THE BRITISH MUSEUM

The plane ride to London is a quiet one. Almost everyone is asleep. It's the perfect time to do more research about the British Museum. You switch on your overhead light and start reading.

Turn the page.

The British Museum was originally housed in Montagu House in 1759. The current building was constructed in its place from 1823 to 1852. During World War II (1939–1945), the museum closed. Many of its priceless objects were moved into tunnels beneath London. From September 1940 to April 1941, the museum was bombed several times. After the war, the building was eventually repaired.

You wonder if you'll encounter anything otherworldly at the museum. It's best to know what you're walking into. You read more about some of the hauntings. A so-called "haunted" mummy-board curses anyone who touches it. Visitors have reported sudden cold spots and ghostly crying. Some have even claimed that unseen hands pushed them! You shudder. You hope no ghostly hands bother you while you're visiting.

When you arrive in London, you take a cab to the British Museum. The city glows with the early morning sun. Soon, the museum comes into view. It's a Greek revival style building with 44 columns along the front. Each column is 45 feet (14 meters) tall.

After paying the driver, you climb the stone stairs and head inside. Your first stop is the Great Court. This massive indoor space has a huge glass roof overhead. In the center is the famous round Reading Room. Famous scholars such as Karl Marx and Virginia Woolf studied there.

It's a busy morning with lots of visitors milling about. With so much to see, you're not sure where to start!

Turn the page.

In college, your great-aunt studied England during the Middle Ages. She suggested you visit Room 41 where she used to work. There, items from an ancient royal Anglo-Saxon burial mound are displayed. The Anglo-Saxon people ruled parts of England and Wales from the 400s to 1066. The burial items were dug up in Suffolk, England, in 1939. The items include a sword and a helmet. You're especially interested in the helmet. One of your characters wears a helmet while fighting a monster. Maybe you can model your fictional helmet off this one.

But you're also itching to see the Rosetta Stone. You are a huge fan of ancient Egypt. One of your novel's characters is too. Without the stone's discovery, historians might never have figured out hieroglyphs. Which place will you visit first?

The Montagu House in the 1800s

- To explore the items in Room 41, turn to page 52.
- To see the famous Rosetta Stone, turn to page 57.

Room 41 is located on the museum's second floor. Heavy wooden doors lead into the large space. The doors have been propped open. When you step inside, you can almost feel the history.

In 1939, a woman named Edith Pretty owned land in Suffolk, England. She was curious about the large earth mounds on her land. She had a local archaeologist investigate. They discovered the mounds were used for burials.

The imprint of a royal Anglo-Saxon ship was found in the mound. The ship would have been 88.5 feet (27 m) long. The wooden ship had rotted away by the time of its discovery. But the items inside were found intact. Inside the ship was a burial chamber loaded with treasures.

You look at display cases holding silver spoons and bowls. A gold-and-garnet purse and gold belt buckle catch your eye.

Soon, you stand face-to-face with an iron helmet from the burial mound. Gold has been hammered into a small mustache over the mouth. A sign says the helmet may have belonged to a king! The helmet's dark, empty eye holes make you feel uneasy.

Suddenly, the temperature of the room drops. Your skin grows cold. Did someone turn up the air-conditioning? You shiver.

A cold wind whips across the back of your body. The floor moves a little under your feet. It almost feels as if someone has run behind you. But when you turn around, no one's there.

- To keep exploring the room, turn to page 54.
- To leave Room 41 and find the Rosetta Stone, turn to page 57.

When you move away from the helmet, the cold disappears. When you step closer, it returns. You're officially weirded out and decide to move on to the next display case.

As you walk along, you notice that the doors to the exhibit are closed. Funny, they were open only a moment ago. You never heard anyone shut them, and the other visitors are gone.

You try to open the gallery doors. They open a few inches and stop.

"Hello?" you call out. "Can someone help me? The doors are stuck!"

Suddenly, something slams into your chest. It feels almost like . . . a hand. You're thrown backward into the gallery. You land on your back. All the air is knocked out of your chest.

Once you can breathe again, you stand. The heavy doors are now standing open. Other people are in the gallery. No one seems to have noticed your fall. Keeping your head down, you quickly leave the gallery.

The farther you get from Room 41, the calmer you feel. Maybe the air-conditioning system wasn't working and that's why it got so cold. Still, that doesn't explain the doors, the invisible hand pushing you, or the people disappearing and reappearing. Maybe this museum really is haunted.

You sit on a bench and write it all down in your notebook. This spooky experience might be useful for your novel. Once you finish writing, you head toward the Rosetta Stone.

Turn the page.

After a few steps, you overhear a woman talking about a dog sculpture in the Africa galleries.

"It gave me such a strange feeling," she tells the man next to her. "Almost like it was . . . watching me."

A chill crawls up your back. A dog sculpture that comes to life could make a great addition to your story. But are you brave enough to visit the Africa galleries?

- To go see the Rosetta Stone, go to page 57.
- To view the dog sculpture, turn to page 68.

You reach the Rosetta Stone in the Egyptian sculpture room. The stone was discovered in July 1799 in Egypt. Historians believe French soldiers in Napoleon Bonaparte's army found it. The stone is a broken part of a larger slab.

Rows of small letters are carved into the stone. They are three types of writing—ancient Greek, hieroglyphs, and an Egyptian writing called Demotic. Historians used the stone to decode ancient Egyptian hieroglyphs.

Turn the page.

The Rosetta Stone

A glass case protects the slab. You smile. Seeing the stone in person is a dream come true.

Soon, someone stops behind you. Their reflection is visible in the glass. The person moves closer. A strange sense of unease slithers up your back. Why are they standing so close? You turn around, but there's no one there!

You tour the rest of the sculpture room. Your pulse slows as you view the amazing Egyptian art. Whatever you think you saw in the glass was probably nothing.

Your phone buzzes with a text from your great-aunt. She asks if you've seen the "cursed" mummy-board yet. It's upstairs in the Egyptian mummies gallery. You know curses aren't real. But you're curious and decide to investigate.

A marble staircase leads to the second floor. As you take the stairs, footsteps pound behind you. When you stop, the footsteps stop. Slowly, you look behind you. There's no one there.

That's strange, you think to yourself.

When you face forward, something odd catches your eye. A hazy light appears at the top of the stairs. It looks like a ball of glowing light. You rub your eyes. But the light is still there. You feel a little spooked by it.

- To continue upstairs to see the mummy-board, turn to page 60.
- To hurry back downstairs, turn to page 66.

As you climb a few more stairs, the light takes on an orb-like shape. You try to keep going. But fear has you rooted to the ground.

Footsteps sound behind you again, and you turn back. This time, a man is coming up the stairs. He stops next to you and snaps a photo of the orb. The moment his flash goes off, the orb disappears.

"Scared off another ghost," the man says, disappointed.

He turns to you and introduces himself as Nigel. He's a ghost hunter collecting stories for his local ghost-hunting group. He shows you a small, handheld device.

"This is an EMF meter," Nigel explains. "It detects changes in the electromagnetic field. Ghosts can make big disturbances to the field."

An EMF meter

You're glad you're no longer alone in the stairwell. You tell him you're writing a novel about a magical museum.

"The basement storage rooms have a ton of paranormal activity," Nigel says excitedly. "I know someone who can sneak me down there! Would you like to tag along? It might spark some good ideas for your book."

- To continue to the mummy-board, turn to page 62.
- To sneak into the basement storage rooms with Nigel, turn to page 64.

You don't feel right about sneaking somewhere you don't belong. You head to the Egyptian mummies gallery. You stop to admire the mummy-board your great-aunt told you about. The board is made of wood and painted plaster. It was made around 950 BC. In ancient Egypt, a mummy-board was placed on top of the mummy. The mummy was then placed inside two wooden coffins.

According to legend, four English travelers in Egypt bought this mummy-board in the mid-1800s. A so-called "curse" soon took effect. Everyone who took possession of it was met with terrible luck.

Suddenly, you start to feel strange, almost like there's a buzzing inside your body. As you wander away, the mummy-board's black eyes seem to follow you. You're not sure what's happening. But you don't feel safe in this gallery. Maybe it's time to leave.

Nigel stands near the door snapping more photos. He hasn't left yet for the basement storage rooms. You could still go with him.

Your stomach rumbles. You haven't had lunch yet. Maybe that's why you feel so strange. A good meal might help you feel less afraid.

- To join Nigel, turn to page 64.
- To grab some lunch, turn to page 71.

You and Nigel head downstairs. Nigel leads you to the basement doors. A security guard quickly unlocks them for you.

"I'll give you fifteen minutes," the man says. "Don't make me regret this."

You and Nigel slip through the doors. They close softly behind you as you descend into the basement of the British Museum.

"What kinds of hauntings have been reported down here?" you ask nervously.

Nigel holds his EMF meter in front of him. "Lights turning off by themselves. Alarms going off for no reason. That sort of thing."

That doesn't sound so bad. You move slowly down the shadowed hall. The walls are made of stone. Bare light bulbs hang from the ceiling.

Suddenly, an object hits you in the temple and lands on the floor. You find a small pebble next to your feet. You pick it up, puzzled. Where did it come from? There's no one else down here other than Nigel. Soon, another pebble hits you!

"Nigel!" you call out as you duck around a corner. "Any ghosts down here known for throwing pebbles?"

Nigel joins you. His eyes are huge. "That's another reported haunting," he says. "An employee was in the storage rooms for Greek and Roman sculptures. A pebble flew sideways into his head!"

Suddenly, Nigel's EMF meter begins to blink. Could a ghost be nearby?

- To follow Nigel into one of the storage rooms, turn to page 73.
- To run back upstairs, turn to page 75.

You aren't sure what that light is. And you don't want to find out. You go back the way you came. Footsteps still sound behind you. A quick glance over your shoulder shows you're alone on the stairs.

Your heart rate speeds up as you scramble down the remaining stairs. But your feet tangle up, and you tumble the last few steps. Pain shoots into your ankle. You must have sprained it.

The footsteps on the stairs sound again. You close your eyes, too afraid to look.

"Help!" you cry. You keep your eyes closed until a security guard finds you. You're taken to the hospital for an X-ray and a brace. Your trip to the British Museum has ended, but you won't ever forget it.

THE END

To follow another path, turn to page 16.
To learn more about haunted museums, turn to page 103.

You reach the Africa galleries. Inside are hundreds of objects from the continent. A mask made by the Sungu people catches your eye. A sign says it is made of wood and monkey skin. The long beard is made of a plant called raffia. Historians believe the mask was worn during special ceremonies.

Finally, you find the dog sculpture. The wood and metal object has two heads. It was made in the Congo in the 1800s. Nails and twisted pieces of metal stick up from its back.

Just looking at the statue gives you the creeps. The longer you look, the more you get the feeling this statue is alive. You lean toward the glass case and tap on it once.

You're about to walk away when the dog turns its heads toward you. Its tongues move. Both heads bare their teeth.

The alarms start to blare. It's so loud you must cover your ears. You back away in horror as the dog rams one of its heads into the case. The case cracks. The dog rams into it again. This time, it shatters.

You don't wait around to see what the dog will do next. You sprint out of the gallery. The sound of metal hitting the floor is louder than the alarms. You push yourself faster. But then something chomps onto the back of your leg. You scream in pain as you collapse. Blood pours from your leg.

"Can I help you?" someone asks.

A museum staff member stands over you. The alarms suddenly stop sounding.

Turn the page.

You look at your leg. The dog sculpture is gone. You quickly hike up your pant leg. There are no bite marks or blood.

"No, that can't be right," you say.

You scramble up and hurry to the display case. The dog sculpture is back on its shelf. The case is unbroken.

Your imagination must be running away with you. You head back to your hotel. After brushing your teeth, you change into your pajamas. As you fold your pants, you notice something on the leg. You hold it closer to your face.

Your heart hammers in your chest. On your pant leg are chew marks.

THE END

To follow another path, turn to page 16.
To learn more about haunted museums, turn to page 103.

As you turn to leave, you accidentally bump into the mummy-board display case. A strange jolt shoots into your body, like static electricity. You quickly leave the gallery to head to the café for some lunch.

But the moment you walk through the gallery door, something odd happens. You find yourself standing back in front of the mummy-board. You shake your head. That can't be right. You leave the gallery again, only to find yourself back where you were.

This can't be happening. Soon, four ghostly figures appear. They are dressed in old-timey clothing. They give you sad looks. These must be the people who brought the cursed board back to England.

Turn the page.

You slowly back away from the ghosts. That's when you notice someone lying on the gallery floor. Paramedics are trying to revive the person. It's you!

You must have had a heart attack when you touched the mummy-board display case. Now, your ghost is trapped at the British Museum forever.

THE END

To follow another path, turn to page 16.
To learn more about haunted museums, turn to page 103.

You follow Nigel into the nearest unlocked storage room. A single light bulb casts the space in eerie shadows. Boxes and crates of items fill the room. It will make a perfect setting in your novel. You're glad you came down here.

Soon, something flickers up ahead. A man comes into focus. He's wearing a green apron and bent over an old-fashioned desk. It looks as if he's writing something.

You tap Nigel's shoulder and point to what must be a security guard. Any minute he will notice you and toss you out of the museum. Before you and Nigel can come up with a plan, the man vanishes!

Suddenly, all the lights go out. It's pitch black.

"Nigel?" you whisper. He doesn't answer.

Turn the page.

A breeze flits across the back of your neck. Then you feel something reach into your chest and wrap around your spine. Pain tears through your body. Your legs go wobbly, and you fall to the ground.

The lights snap back on. The security guard who snuck you downstairs frowns at you. "Your time is up," he says, hauling you to your feet.

"What about Nigel?" You look around, but you don't see him. He must have already gone upstairs.

"Who's Nigel?" the man asks. "You're the only one I let down here."

Your heart races. Did you just explore the British Museum with one of its ghostly inhabitants?

THE END

To follow another path, turn to page 16.
To learn more about haunted museums, turn to page 103.

As the EMF meter lights up, you feel something move against the back of your neck.

"I'm out of here!" you shout.

You've seen enough spooky things for one day. You leave Nigel and scurry back upstairs. The lights flicker as you run.

As soon as you leave the basement, you feel better. The British Museum has given you plenty of story ideas. Now you need a nap.

Turn the page.

The bus ride back to your hotel doesn't take long. You get the key from the front desk and go to your room. It's small, but the bed is soft. You quickly change into your pajamas and climb into bed. Your feet brush against something in the sheets. You slowly peel back the covers.

Inside your sheets are dozens of pebbles, just like from the museum.

THE END

To follow another path, turn to page 16.
To learn more about haunted museums, turn to page 103.

CHAPTER 4
THE SMITHSONIAN

As your bus heads toward the Smithsonian in Washington, D.C., you research the museum. The Smithsonian has 17 museums, galleries, and a zoo. There are more than 150 million objects to discover. It's a bit overwhelming. You're meeting Colin's sister, Adrien, at the Museum of Natural History this afternoon. But this morning, you're on your own.

Turn the page.

The Castle was the first Smithsonian building. Today, it's a visitor's center. It might be a great place to start. As you read, you learn many people died in the building. Scientist Fielding Meek died there in 1876. Joseph Henry, the Smithsonian's first secretary, lived in the Castle with this family. His son William died there in 1862. Joseph himself died in the Castle in 1878.

Since then, there have been stories of ghostly visitors to the Castle. In 1900, a night watchman said he saw Joseph Henry's ghost. His spirit was rumored to be guarding the Castle.

In the 1970s, the hauntings increased. A woman said invisible hands grabbed her necklace. Books fell from the shelves by themselves. Since then, people have reported ghostly screams and strange noises throughout the building.

You also plan to visit the Smithsonian's National Museum of American History. This museum opened in January 1964. At first, it was called the National Museum of History and Technology. Today, many famous objects are housed there, including the Star-Spangled Banner flag. A Kermit the Frog puppet from *Sesame Street* also calls this museum home.

You read that there might also be a haunting inhabitant. A ghostly man in a military jacket has been spotted in one of the stairwells. He stands near the exhibit on American Wars. One of your book characters is a World War II hero. This exhibit might be worth checking out. You're not so sure about the ghost.

Turn the page.

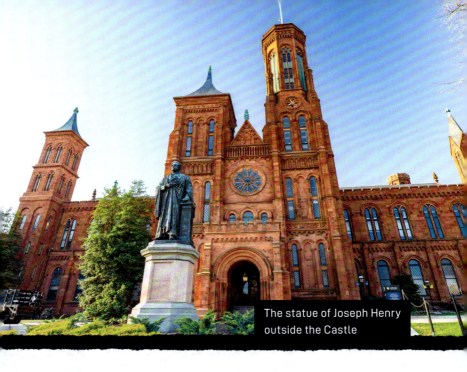

The statue of Joseph Henry outside the Castle

Finally, your bus arrives in the nation's capital city. You stare out the window as you pass by the White House and the Capitol Building. Soon, the bus turns toward the Smithsonian museums. Which will you choose to visit first?

- To visit the Castle first, go to page 83.
- To head to the National Museum of American History, turn to page 89.

The bus drops you in front of the Castle. The building is made of red sandstone and has a clock tower. A large statue of a man seems to guard the museum. A plaque says it's Joseph Henry.

You're about to head inside when something moves at the bottom of the statue. It might be a leaf or a squirrel. You move closer. The stone fabric of Henry's robe seems to ripple, as if flapping in the breeze.

Joseph Henry

Turn the page.

I must be imagining it, you tell yourself. *Statues can't move.*

As you step away, a shadow-like figure slowly grows out of the statue. It hovers above the stone. It almost looks like . . . a man. Then it slips back into the stone.

There are clouds in the sky. Maybe it's just a shadow from the sunlight and clouds. But you're a little creeped out. Maybe you should skip the Castle.

- To continue into the Castle anyway, go to page 85.
- To go straight to the Museum of American History, turn to page 89.

Inside, the Castle has glass displays along the walls and towering stone ceilings. Soon, you find yourself at the crypt of James Smithson, founder of the Smithsonian. The crypt contains his original gravestone from Genoa, Italy. Smithson's bones are kept underneath it. In 1974, the founder's bones were dug up and studied. Smithson's body has been disturbed many times.

A cold breeze sweeps through the room. Goose bumps break out on your skin. These old buildings are drafty. Still, you get the feeling you're being watched and quickly leave.

You continue to the Great Hall. Visitors walk about, and you're glad to be around other people. A sign says that in 1850, the floor in the Great Hall began to sink. A large part of the hall fell into the basement. Luckily, no one was injured.

Turn the page.

To save money, wooden columns and rafters had been used instead of iron and bricks when the building was built. That's why the room sank.

The Hall had different uses over the years. At first, it housed natural history specimens, including dinosaur bones. Later, it became a public library. Today, there is a café and gift shop in the Hall.

As you approach the gift shop, something cracks overhead. The floor rumbles. No one else seems to feel or hear whatever is happening. But you're afraid the Hall is about to collapse again!

A man in a fancy suit strides past. He seems to be inspecting the building. But he doesn't seem afraid. He might know what's going on.

- To ask the man what's happening, go to page 87.
- To warn everyone to flee the Hall, go to page 94.

The man's suit is very old-fashioned. He looks over every nook and cranny of the Hall. He must work here.

"Excuse me, sir," you say, and he turns to face you. "Do you know why the building is rumbling?"

The man takes out a gold pocket watch and checks it. "We're terribly behind schedule," he says.

You're confused. "Is the museum closing early today?" you ask. The sign said it was open for several more hours.

The man shakes his head. "Construction is behind, I'm afraid. The Hall was to be ready months ago."

The man looks a bit familiar. You wonder if you've met before. Slowly, you recognize the man's face. You just saw it on the statue outside.

Turn the page.

"W-what's your name?" you ask, afraid you already know the answer.

The man holds out a hand. "I'm Mr. Joseph Henry, secretary of this grand institution. And what is your name?"

You can't believe what you're seeing. Is your mind playing tricks on you? Maybe you should shake it off and head to the Museum of American History. Or should you reach out to this apparition in front of you?

- To flee and go to the Museum of American History, go to page 89.
- To shake Joseph Henry's ghostly hand, turn to page 96.

The Museum of American History sits on the other side of the National Mall. The Mall's large green space is the perfect place for a morning stroll. You stop at the Lincoln Memorial and the Washington Monument.

Soon, you arrive at the Museum of American History. Marble covers the front of this modern building. You spend a few hours touring this fascinating place. President Abraham Lincoln's top hat is on display. It's the hat he wore the night he was killed.

You stop in front of a pair of glittering red shoes. They are the ruby slippers Judy Garland wore in the 1939 film *The Wizard of Oz*. You send a photo to your great-aunt. It's her favorite movie.

Turn the page.

Finally, you take the staircase to the exhibit on American wars. After only a few steps, you start to feel ill at ease. Your pulse races. You stop halfway between floors and glance up.

A man in a green military jacket from World War II (1939–1945) leans against a banister. You wonder if he's part of the World War II exhibit. He might have some good information you could use in your novel. Still, there's something strange about him. Could he be the ghostly soldier you read about?

Suddenly, your phone buzzes with a text from Colin's sister, Adrien. She has just arrived at the Natural History Museum. She wonders if you would like to have lunch together.

- To have lunch at the Natural History Museum, go to page 91.
- To approach the man on the stairs, turn to page 97.

There's something odd about the man in the military jacket. You turn and quickly go back down the stairs. When you look behind you, the man is gone. You never heard a door open or close.

The Natural History Museum is next door. This museum opened in 1910. It houses 148 million artifacts and specimens. A stuffed African elephant greets you in the museum's rotunda. A sign says his name is Henry. He first went on display in 1959.

Adrien waits for you nearby. "How have the museums been so far?" she asks.

You swallow and tell her your haunting experiences.

"I haven't seen any ghosts yet," she admits. "But I've heard stories."

Turn the page.

After lunch, Adrien takes you to see the Hope Diamond. The famous blue stone glitters in its case.

"Anyone who touches it is said to be cursed," Adrien says.

In 1958, a mail carrier named James Todd delivered the diamond to the museum. Within a year, Todd broke his leg, his wife died, and his house burned down.

"Do you think the curse is real?" you ask.

Adrien shrugs. "I'm not sure."

You turn back to the case. It's hard to imagine something so beautiful could cause such bad luck.

You suddenly need to use the restroom. Adrien takes you into the staff quarters near the Hope Diamond.

"These bathrooms are less busy," she says. "I'll wait here for you."

You slip into one of the bathrooms. It's empty. It has wooden doors on the stalls and faucets you turn by hand at the sinks. As you shut yourself into a stall, a faucet turns on.

Someone must have come in, you tell yourself.

"Adrien?" you ask. "Are you in here?"
No one answers.

When you leave the stall, no one's there. You wash your hands and turn off the faucet.

Must be bad plumbing, you tell yourself.

Suddenly, the faucet at the sink next to you turns on. The faucet handle moved by itself!

- To turn off the faucet, turn to page 99.
- To run away and find Adrien, turn to page 101.

You scramble through the Great Hall. "Get out!" you shout. "The Hall is about to collapse!"

People give you strange looks. They start to whisper. Why isn't anyone listening to you?

Suddenly, the Hall changes. The lights are dimmer. The walls are dark wood. The people are gone. Shelves contain specimens of animals and insects. A giant dinosaur skeleton towers above you. It wasn't there a moment ago. None of this was.

The floor shakes and cracks, and you fall onto your back. The dinosaur bones begin dropping to the ground. You roll out of the way just as the skull hits the ground. Dust flies everywhere. The floor falls out from underneath you. You scream as you fall into the basement of the Castle. Everything goes dark.

When you wake up, you're outside again. The sun shines brightly. Birds sing. You slowly look up. You're standing in front of Joseph Henry's statue. Your whole body goes cold as you check the time on your phone.

Only one minute has passed since you got off the bus. When the bus returns, you clamber up the steps. You're ready to leave this haunted museum.

THE END

To follow another path, turn to page 16.
To learn more about haunted museums, turn to page 103.

Slowly, you reach for Mr. Henry's hand. Your heart thuds in your chest. You can't believe you're about to shake hands with a ghost! The writer in you is too curious not to try.

Just as you reach for him, your hand passes through his. Coldness seeps into your skin. It feels like you've plunged your arm into a bucket of ice water.

Joseph Henry dissolves, as if he was made of smoke. None of the other visitors seem to have noticed him.

You quickly take out your notebook. You write down everything about your encounter with this famous Smithsonian ghost. He might make a great character in your novel!

THE END

To follow another path, turn to page 16.
To learn more about haunted museums, turn to page 103.

As you climb the stairs, the man remains at the banister. Slowly, he makes eye contact with you. But your body freezes with fear. That's when you notice the man's body looks kind of hazy. All the sound in the stairwell disappears. You can't even hear yourself breathe.

The door to the war exhibit opens. Some people step out. When you look at the banister, the man is gone. Did you only imagine him? Or did you have an otherworldly experience?

"Are you alright?" a woman asks you. "You look like you've seen a ghost."

"I'm fine," you mumble and hurry past her into the exhibit.

The Americans at War exhibit is large. Objects from the nation's many wars are on display.

Turn the page.

You stop to admire George Washington's sword. He led the Continental army during the Revolutionary War (1775–1783). He also became the nation's first president.

Up ahead, a World War II Jeep hangs from the ceiling. Display cases hold military uniforms and weapons from that time.

One uniform looks familiar. You realize it's just like the one worn by the man you saw. As you move closer, you study old black-and-white photos. You focus on one.

In this photo is the young soldier you just saw. He's wearing the same military jacket. Your blood runs cold. You really did just see a ghost.

THE END

To follow another path, turn to page 16.
To learn more about haunted museums, turn to page 103.

You quickly turn off the faucet. But then the next faucet handle turns. As soon as you turn it off, the next handle moves. Water gushes into the sink. You turn it off and stand perfectly still. Your heart races. Is the plumbing bad? Or is this bathroom haunted?

Suddenly, the toilets start flushing. You try to open the bathroom door, but it's stuck.

"Help!" you scream as water gushes onto the floor. It reaches your feet, then rises to cover your ankles. You pound on the door, begging for someone to help you.

Suddenly, the door opens. A woman stands on the other side. She wears a name tag.

"The water!" you cry. "It wouldn't shut off!"

Turn the page.

The woman looks into the bathroom and frowns. You look at your feet. There's no water anywhere.

"I swear there was water everywhere!" you tell her.

"This area is for staff only," she says and calls for security on her walkie-talkie. Your Smithsonian visit has been cut short. But at least you got lots of good ideas for your novel!

THE END

To follow another path, turn to page 16.
To learn more about haunted museums, turn to page 103.

You run back into the main exhibition space. Adrien asks you what's wrong, but you're having trouble catching your breath. The room spins, and your stomach aches. You suddenly feel the need to leave the museum. You swear the Hope Diamond glows brighter as you rush past it.

You stumble down to the main floor and dash out the doors. As soon as you're outside, your dizziness goes away.

At your hotel, you shower and get ready for bed. The spooky events at the Smithsonian have left you rattled. You climb under the covers, still haunted by what happened in the bathroom.

You're about to fall asleep when the sound of the faucet turning on in the bathroom jolts you awake.

THE END

To follow another path, turn to page 16.
To learn more about haunted museums, turn to page 103.

CHAPTER 5
HAUNTED MUSEUMS

Museums are homes to objects and artwork from around the world and across time. Some pieces are donated to museums. Some museums display stolen artifacts. Other items have tragic histories. All this history might explain why so many people believe museums are haunted places.

Some of the ghostly stories are probably just that—stories. At the Louvre, a novel inspired the story of the mummy ghost. The novel *Belphégor* by Arthur Bernède was published in 1927. In the book, a masked man pretends to be a "mummy" haunting the Louvre. After reading the book, some visitors let their imaginations run wild. The story was re-told many times. Visitors may have started to believe it.

But some haunting tales are rooted in true stories. In March 1850, William H. Page was the first person to die at the Smithsonian. He was working to repair the Castle building when he fell off scaffolding. He wouldn't be the last to die there. There was even a murder at the Arts and Industries building in 1907. Death can be scary to talk about. Ghost stories can help people deal with their fears. But does that mean the Smithsonian is truly haunted?

At the British Museum, the ghostly stories of Room 41 were caught on tape. A guard reported locking the room. Soon, the doors were suddenly wide open again. None of the other doors nearby opened. The guard watched security footage that showed the doors opening on their own.

The Louvre, British Museum, and Smithsonian house some of the world's most priceless artifacts. Some people say these museums have something supernatural in their collections. From ghostly workers to mummies that move on their own, these experiences have spooked visitors.

But how can hauntings be proven? Ghost hunters use lots of tools to try to prove ghosts are real. But so far, no one has proven that ghosts exist.

More Ghostly Encounters

Cleaners at the British Museum reported the mummies moving when they polished their display cases. They said the fabric wrapping would start to ripple. After that, many cleaners refused to clean the cases. Museum staff thought the cleaners must have scrubbed the cases too hard. Others said a buildup of static electricity made the fabric move. New cleaners were hired.

The ghost of a little red man has made several appearances at the Louvre. He appeared to France's King Henry IV right before he died in 1610. His ghost also visited King Louis XVI twice in 1792. First, a cleaning woman claimed she found a gnome-like man wearing red in the king's bed. A few months later, guards said a man in red was in the king's prison cell. Was it Jack the Skinner's ghost?

A ghostly zookeeper is said to haunt the Smithsonian Zoo. He visits the elephant enclosure at night. One museum worker said the ghost looked at her and then faded away. Some believe it might be the ghost of William Blackburne. He was the zoo's first head zookeeper. He walked the first elephants into the zoo.

Other Paths to Explore

1. If you worked at the Louvre, British Museum, or Smithsonian, would you believe the ghost stories? What would you do if you had a ghostly encounter of your own? Would you tell visitors? Do you think the ghostly stories would attract or distract visitors?

2. James Smithson's bones are kept at the Smithsonian. Do you think the presence of his bones caused some of the ghostly tales? If workers removed his bones, would the so-called hauntings stop?

3. The Louvre was a royal palace before it was a museum. Millions of people have passed through the Louvre. Do you think all that history makes people more or less likely to believe it's haunted?

Glossary

ancient (AYN-shunt)—from a long time ago

artifact (AR-tuh-fakt)—an object used in the past that was made by people

electromagnetic field (i-lek-troh-mag-NET-ik FEELD)—a field of force created by moving electric charges

fortress (FOR-tris)—a place such as a castle that is protected against attack

hieroglyphs (HYE-ruh-glifs)—pictures or symbols used in the ancient Egyptian system of writing

paranormal (pair-uh-NOR-muhl)—having to do with an unexplained event that has no scientific explanation

sarcophagus (sar-KAH-fuh-guhs)—a stone coffin; the ancient Egyptians placed inner coffins into a sarcophagus

scaffolding (SKAF-ol-ding)—temporary framework or a set of platforms used to support workers and materials

supernatural (soo-pur-NACH-ur-uhl)—something that cannot be explained by science

Select Bibliography

Angell, Noah. *Ghosts of the British Museum: A True Story of Colonial Loot and Restless Objects.* London: Monoray, an imprint of Octopus Publishing Group Ltd, 2024.

Klimek, Chris. "The Ghosts Who Haunt the Smithsonian." *Smithsonian Magazine.* smithsonianmag.com/smithsonian-institution/the-ghosts-who-haunt-the-smithsonian-180981013/ Accessed July 2, 2024.

Ogden, Tom. *Haunted Washington, D.C.: Federal Phantoms, Government Ghosts, and Beltway Banshees.* Guildford, CT: Globe Pequot, 2016.

Steiger, Brad. *Real Ghosts, Restless Spirits, and Haunted Places.* Canton, MI: Visible Ink Press, 2013.

"The Haunted Louvre: the Three Ghosts that Inhabit the World's Most Famous Museum." *Amazing Museum News.* amazingmuseums.news/blog/the-haunted-louvre:-the-3-ghosts-that-inhabit-the-world's-most-famous-museum/ Accessed July 2, 2024.

Read More

Harvey, Jeanne Walker. *The Glass Pyramid: A Story of the Louvre and Architect I.M. Pei.* New York: Antheneum Books for Young Readers, 2025.

Markovics, Joyce L. *Scary Museums.* Minneapolis: Bearport Publishing Company, 2021.

Mooney, Carla. *Ghost Sightings.* San Diego, CA: BrightPoint Press, 2024.

Internet Sites

British Museum Ghosts: An Insider's Guide to Its Hauntings
spookyisles.com/british-museum-ghosts/#google_vignette

Busting 13 of the Smithsonian's Most Persistent Myths
smithsonianmag.com/smithsonian-institution/busting-13-of-the-smithsonians-most-persistent-myths-135407460/

Get Inspired at the Louvre
louvre.fr/en/

About the Author

Megan Cooley Peterson is a children's book author and editor. Her book *How to Build Hair-Raising Haunted Houses* (Capstone Press, 2011) was selected as a Book of Note by the TriState Young Adult Review Committee. When not writing, Megan enjoys movies, books, and all things Halloween. She lives in Minnesota with her husband and daughter.